Nine Months to A Miracle

A KEEPSAKE FOR THE MOTHER-TO-BE

Leslie Carola

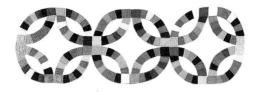

Longmeadow Press

For Maria and Matthew, miracles of the highest order.

This book is intended as a reference volume only, not as a medical manual or guide to self-treatment. It is not intended as a substitute for the medical advice of physicians. The reader should regularly consult a physician in general, and particularly when pregnant. If you are pregnant or think that you are pregnant, we urge you to seek competent medical help. Keep in mind that exercise and nutritional needs vary from person to person, depending on age, health, status or individual variations. The information here is intended to help you make informed decisions about your health, not as a substitue for any treatment that may have been prescribed by your doctor.

Copyright © 1991 by Arena Books

Prepared by Arena Books. All spot illustrations in this book are details from quilts, courtesy of America Hurrah, New York, NY.

ISBN 0-681-41157-0

Printed in Singapore
9 8 7 6 5 4 3 2 1

Contents

Introduction

*Pregnancy and birth. One cannot help but stand in
awe at the miracle of it. To be part of it is the most
exhilarating, exciting experience of a woman's
lifetime. It is a time to be cherished and remembered.*

*Pregnancy is at the same time unique to each woman, and universally
shared. It is a deeply emotional journey that is both joyful and
complicated. To feel ambivalent about it at some point during the course
of your pregnancy is perfectly normal. It means that you are aware of
the magnitude of it all. The responsibilities are awesome, and your life
will change permanently.*

*A woman expecting a child has a real need to share her feelings with
others. Your sense of who you are, how you and your body react, the
joy and the stress you feel are instantaneous and important. If you take*

the time to write it down, you have given yourself a keepsake for all time. One that you may even wish to share with your child.

Many women have said that although they were glad to be rid of the discomfort of the last month or so of pregnancy, they missed the incredible intimacy, the privacy of the baby within them. But while you are participating in giving this great gift, the gift of life, you can acquire a greater understanding of yourself and others.

Carrying a child and giving birth demands the highest physical and emotional energy. Each month your body responds appropriately to the increasing demands placed on it by the developing baby. At the end of the nine months, you are ready psychologically and physically to release the child. Each step unfolds naturally, in its own time, in its own rhythm.

A pregnant woman's midnight cravings/longings for unusual foods or combinations of foods are legendary. There may be valid reason for craving certain foods, but long ago it was believed that if a pregnant woman's longings were not satisfied the baby would be imperfect. These edible yearnings were taken so seriously that "longing" became a euphemism for "pregnant." The desire for out-of-season fruit or any unusual delicacy became proof itself of pregnancy.

*The
First
Trimester*

You Are Pregnant

It's been confirmed. You are pregnant. *It may be what you have been hoping for and dreaming about for years. It may be a total shock. It may not be what you wanted right now. But in less than a year, you will be a mother. You have time to get used to the idea. And marvel at the way your body adapts to the needs of the developing infant.*

In many ways, the first few months of pregnancy are the most confusing and unsettling. You do need time to get used to the idea, even if you have been anticipating it. The reality of it can be numbing at first. But so can winning the lottery! There is joy and anticipation perhaps mixed with a wistfulness for your own lost childhood, and great hope for the new person.

For the next nine months you will think about every activity, mundane or not, in terms of its safety for the developing baby who is totally dependent on you. You need this time -- the nine months -- to find the balance between being a woman and a mother. The more in tune you are with the process the easier it will be to make the transition to mother. And if you find the balance with your partner now, it will be more pleasurable to make the transition to parents together.

There are many physical demands placed on you during these nine months. Exercise, rest, relaxation, and nutrition play critical roles in the successful pregnancy. You may need more rest now than you are used to getting; you may feel sleepy frequently during the first

three months. Your body has to adapt to the needs of the baby.

The Baby

F rom a single fertilized egg an embryo forms which will be
*about the size of a pea by the end of the first month. And eight
months from now you will have a full-size baby. It is very normal to be in
awe of this whole phenomenon.*

Your Reactions

T his is a special time for you and your partner. You may want
*some privacy to savor it. Think about keeping the good news to
yourselves for a while. Once you do tell people your life takes on a whole
new dimension.*

A *lthough you are not aware of the baby's development in the
first month, you may wish to record some dates here. When was
your first doctor's appointment? How do you feel about your doctor?*

_____

_____

_____

W *hat was your first reaction to the news of your pregnancy?
Who did you tell? How did they react?*

_____

_____

_____

Diet & Nutrition

Develop a sensible eating plan, with the advice of your doctor, right away. Concentrate on foods that provide optimum nutrition for the baby and for you. Your overall goal should be to gain about 25 pounds gradually over the nine months. You need extra protein, vitamins, calcium and iron. You will do well if you eat a sensible diet, adding an extra 300 calories a day for the developing baby.

Your Body

A woman needs to be in prime physical condition to give birth to her baby. Check with your doctor to develop a personal program that fits your exercise requirements and lifestyle. This might lead to lifetime fitness. Remember, it is important to get plenty of rest (at least eight hours of sleep at night and an hour's nap in the afternoon).

*G*ive your baby a healthy, nutritious start. Think for two.
How can you improve your diet?

_____

_____

_____

*T*hink of three ways you can slip some exercise into your life
without really trying (get off the bus two blocks before your stop
and walk the rest of the way, for example).

_____

_____

_____

13

The Baby

*T*he baby is now beginning to develop recognizable features. The baby moves around although you can't feel it yet. It is about an inch long, which means it could fit inside a walnut shell. You may want to ask your doctor to recommend a few books on the physical development of the baby.

Your Reactions

*E*motional seesaws are a natural reaction to a major life change. Your initial euphoric reaction to the news of your pregnancy may be tempered by feelings of outright terror: "Am I capable of being a good mother, or ready to be a mother? How involved will my partner be? What will he think of me? How is this baby going to change our relationship?

*Y*ou might talk with other mothers about their experiences
during pregnancy. It is fun to compare notes.

_____

_____

_____

*I*t's a good idea to share your feelings with your partner,
doctor or a close friend, as well as writing them down here.

_____

_____

_____

Diet & Nutrition

*T*he developing baby needs regular nourishment at appropriate intervals. Don't be tempted to skip meals. You could spread your daily food allottment over four or six meals instead of three if that makes you more comfortable. Remember to balance the calories.

Your Body

*Y*ou should be exercising at least 30 minutes a day, three times a week. Swimming and walking are probably the best exercises for you, since they do not put any additional strain on your body. The water supports you when you swim and walking does not require any special balance. Exercising will help you gain aerobic fitness and will help you relax. Avoid high-risk and contact sports.

S top and ask yourself "Is this the best I can do for the baby?" before you bite into any food. Have you added the extra milk the baby needs?

H ow can you fit a 30-minute walk into your day? Put it on your calendar first, and then organize your day around it. You'll look and feel better.

The Baby

B y the end of the month the baby swims, kicks, turns at the end
of the umbilical cord like an astronaut in space. It can swallow.
Don't be afraid to discuss any questions you have with your doctor.
You will be seeing him/her every month and part of the purpose of your
prenatal visits is to make you as comfortable as possible.

Your Reactions

I f you worry about the anticipated weight gain, just remember that
it is temporary. It is not fat, but baby, plus the necessary support
for the baby. You will regain your familiar — and maybe even improved
— shape soon after the birth.

*W*rite down any questions you have for your doctor about the
developing baby.

_____

_____

_____

*Y*ou could take the time now to look through your clothes and
make a checklist of what you might be able to wear through the
rest of your pregnancy.

_____

_____

_____

Diet & Nutrition

*I*t is important to follow your doctor's orders, because taking care of yourself and your baby now will make it easier after the baby is born. Your calorie needs depend on your normal build and weight. Be sure to include enough fiber in your diet now by eating plenty of fresh raw fruits and vegetables, whole grains, and drink lots of water.

Your Body

*C*ontinue walking for exercise for up to 30 minutes a day to develop aerobic strength. And start adding some stretching, relaxing yoga movements. They will help destress your life, and prepare your muscles for the work of labor and delivery as well as build your self-confidence.

S ubstituting fresh fruit for the sugar in your diet is an excellent
*way to eliminate wasted sugar calories and increase your intake of
complex carbohydrates. Where can you adjust your menus?*

_____

_____

_____

H ave you noticed any special side effects, like fuller hair, a
healthier glow to your skin?

_____

_____

A Mbuti mother in Zaire communicates with her unborn baby regularly. She talks to it continually throughout the day, telling it about the forest they live in, naming everyday objects for it, readying herself and the child for their life together. She even sings her own special song created just for the baby. In this process the mother reinforces her own concept of the world, giving herself confidence that the world will be as kind to her child as it has been to her.

The Second Trimester

Looking Your Best

The way you look during pregnancy affects how you feel about yourself. *It also affects the way people respond to you. If you feel good about yourself, you project that self-confidence. Maternity clothes are quite attractive now, and if you didn't wear pink gingham, puff-sleeved tops before you were pregnant, there is no reason to do so now. You do have a choice.*

A professional woman normally takes time to look fashionable and well-groomed before she leaves home in the morning. You can still do that when you are pregnant. In fact, nonprofessional women would do well to follow the same principle. A good, easy haircut, some light, well-applied make-up and a simple dress, suit or pants and jacket will give your spirits a lift. There are even attractive maternity bathing suits available for trips to the beach, or the backyard.

Make the extra effort to look your best during pregnancy. Psychologically, it is very important. You will feel better, and more in control. And your partner will feel better. With all the distressing changes brought about by pregnancy, your partner can feel reassured by seeing you feeling and looking happy and self-confident, and his positive feelings can benefit you.

When you are working, do your best to maintain a professional attitude. If you don't let your pregnancy interfere with your work, no one else will. Handle your pregnancy with the same dignity and professionalism with which you handle everything else in the office. It may be more of a challenge, but you can combine the two worlds effectively.

The Baby

D uring the fourth month the infant grows to a length of up to eight to ten inches -- almost half the length it will be at birth. Now it can, and often does, suck its thumb. Some babies are born with blisters on their thumbs from sucking them before they were born.

Your Reactions

Y our stomach may protrude a bit, and you will certainly have to loosen your clothes. You should feel generally healthy and happy during these next three months. Many women have a renewed sense of energy. You may find that sex becomes freer and more satisfying. Be sure to check with your doctor.

D *o you wonder who your baby will look like, and what it's personality will be?*

_____

_____

_____

P *regnancy is a leap into the unknown, and that can be unsettling. Have you thought of any ways to combat this stress?*

_____

_____

_____

Diet & Nutrition

*I*n addition to eating a nourishing diet, you should avoid caffeine
*and alcohol. And, if you smoke, you must concentrate on stopping
immediately. Anything that you eat or drink or smoke will affect the
baby, and alcohol, caffeine and cigarettes can cause harmful effects.*

Your Body

*Y*our body image -- the way you perceive yourself -- is part of your
essential self-identity. Pregnancy disrupts your body image, but
with regular exercise you can preserve and develop a positive self image.

*W*hat are some of your favorite healthy snacks? How often do you eat them?

_____

_____

_____

*Y*ou can start learning the breathing control necessary for natural childbirth. Slowly start preparing yourself for your baby's birth day.

_____

_____

_____

The Baby

*T*his month you will very likely feel the baby moving for the first time, often when you are resting or lying down. That first nudge can be a very special moment.

Your Reactions

*H*usbands are sometimes confused and wonder if they will ever again be important in their wive's lives. Pregnant wives may feel confused and angry at this, but it is all a normal reaction to the major changes brought about by pregnancy. The fears are real. Share the changes and your feelings with your husband. You are in this together.

*W*hen did you first feel your baby moving? What were you doing? Did it surprise you?

_____

_____

_____

*R*emember to include your partner in your feelings. Talk now while you have the time together.

_____

_____

_____

Diet & Nutrition

*R*eview your diet if you are gaining too much weight (more than 15 pounds so far). Include more fish and skinless chicken in your diet. You can eat red meat, but make sure to trim away any visible fat. Cook meat on a rack so the fat drips off; and use skim milk.

Your Body

*Y*ou will most likely have to start wearing maternity clothes to accommodate your expanding middle. By improving your posture, you can prevent a common problem of pregnancy -- lower back strain. Your doctor will be able to recommend exercises for you.

*K*eep track of what you are eating. It's easier to eliminate or add appropriate foods when you can see a record of what you've been eating.

_____

_____

_____

*T*ry to add another 20 - 30 minutes of exercise three times a week, so that you are walking for 30 minutes in the morning and again in the late afternoon or evening.

_____

_____

_____

The Baby

*H*ave you thought of a name for your baby yet? Are you naming the baby after a special person? The doctor may ask for the name, right after the delivery, to complete the birth certificate. It's good to be prepared!

Your Reactions

*Y*ou might worry that you won't look your best, that your relationship with your husband won't be the same, that you love your job and don't want to give it up. This doesn't mean that you won't be a good mother. It's very important to maintain outside interests while you are pregnant and after the baby is born.

*W*hat are some of the names you are considering? Do you and your partner agree?

_____

_____

_____

_____

_____

*W*hat arrangements have you made for leaving your job — temporarily or permanently?

_____

_____

_____

_____

Diet & Nutrition

*H*ave you tried making your own soup and your own mayonaise? By doing so, you can easily cut down on salt and preservatives. And the taste is far superior to anything you can buy.

Your Body

*T*he extra time you spend walking each day could be a good time for you and your husband to spend together, talking over the changes and anticipations of the next few months.

B *e sure that you are getting plenty of calcium to meet your baby's*
*   needs. What sources of calcium are you taking now?*

_____

_____

_____

_____

O *nce you have mastered an exercise so that it is no longer*
*   challenging, change the position of your body to make it more*
difficult, rather than repeating the exercise.

_____

_____

_____

When an expectant mother from East Siberia goes walking, she must kick away any stones or lumps of earth that lie in her path, to prevent any obstructions during her delivery. Once she has started out for her walk, she must not turn back; otherwise she might cause labor to start and stop before its job is done.

*The
Third
Trimester*

Relaxation Tips

Next to eating well and exercising regularly, *relaxing properly is most important when you are expecting a baby. Pregnancy itself is a stressful situation. You will be transformed from a familiar figure, someone you know to someone unknown, brand new -- a mother. Your relationship with your partner changes, your finances may change, even your home may change. And certainly your body changes, if only temporarily. Clearly, pregnancy provides significant anxiety.*

A healthy way to manage the stress of pregnancy is to practice some kind of yoga, or stretching techniques, in combination with an aerobic exercise like good brisk walking. The exercise program you

develop now could be the basis for a lifelong fitness program from which you will receive wonderful, healthy rewards.

You can combat the effects of stress by learning to listen to yourself, and by developing a relaxation program to answer your own needs. Keeping a journal in which you express the fears, anxieties and highlights of your pregnancy is another way to reduce the stress.

Relaxed women tend to have easier, non-traumatic deliveries, and more comfortable post-delivery periods.

Courtesy America Hurrah

41

The Baby

*T*his may be a good time for you and your partner to draw up a plan to divide the workload once the baby is born. If you don't do it now, you are leaving room for resentment to develop later. Are there any other children? Do you both have jobs outside of the home? Will you continue to work? How much maternity leave will you have?

Your Reactions

*A*s the delivery date gets closer, many women worry about their baby's health, that the baby will be damaged in some way. You can help to alleviate these thoughts by concentrating on thinking of more positive things. Knowing that emotions run high during pregnancy, it is better to identify your reactions and deal with them than to be afraid of the consequences.

*H*ow will you and your partner divide the work? Will you have outside help for the first month with your newborn?

_____

_____

_____

_____

*W*rite down your fears about the baby, and then discuss them with your partner and your doctor.

_____

_____

_____

_____

Diet & Nutrition

*K*eep to a simple diet, avoiding hard-to-digest spicy foods.
Portions should be comfortably small, and frequent enough to
maintain a steady blood sugar level.

Your Body

*Y*ou can prepare for the delivery gently, but consistently. If you
keep up the aerobic conditioning, breathing and stretching
exercises you should be in very good shape for the birth of the baby.

A re any foods bothering you? Make a note each time and see if you can detect a pattern.

_____

_____

_____

_____

E xercise to soothing music, concentrating on breathing properly. Remember to exhale. What is your favorite music to exercise to?

_____

_____

_____

_____

The Baby

*Y*ou have probably realized by now that you alone have provided the ''home,'' the food, and even the entertainment for the developing baby who responds to loud noises or gentle prodding by kicking and moving around. Sometimes when you least expect it, the baby will decide it's time to stretch or kick. Or even hiccup.

Your Reactions

*N*ow is the time to plan your delivery. Will your partner be with you throughout labor and delivery? Have you and your partner discussed it with your doctor? Are you comfortable with the decision?

*W*hat does your baby respond to? Is it more active at any
particular time of day?

_____

_____

_____

_____

*H*ow do you feel when you can **see** the baby kicking and
stretching? Has your partner seen the baby moving yet?

_____

_____

_____

_____

Diet & Nutrition

*D*on't start cutting back on your caloric intake now. You will probably not want to eat much at one sitting, but eat lightly several times a day. And don't forget your milk.

Your Body

*R*emember that soon you will deliver your child and you want to be in peak physical condition to do so. Deliver: from Liberare to free; to set free from restraint. And so you will release your child into the world.

*W*rite down what you are eating so you can be sure you are taking in enough of the essential nutrients.

_____

_____

_____

_____

*H*ave you packed your bag for the hospital yet? You will need your things as well as a few things for the baby -- diapers, receiving blanket, something to wear home.

_____

_____

_____

The Baby

*Y*ou may have mild contractions occasionally throughout the
month, and usually the baby and the whole protruding abdomen
drop lower in preparation for birth. The baby who has been swimming
peacefully in a warm bath, is preparing himself for a difficult journey.

Your Reactions

*A*lthough all women become cumbersome, tired of pregnancy and
anxious about delivery, many develop an overiding inner peace
this last month. This is the time to have a pile of good books at your
side to keep you occupied.

*W*hat are your feelings as you wait this last month.
Try to rest and have a relaxing last few weeks.

_____

_____

_____

_____

*W*hat are you reading? How are you keeping occupied these
last few weeks?

_____

_____

_____

_____

51

Diet & Nutrition

*P*ay special attention to the last few weeks of your diet for two. Generally distract yourself from the impending birth. It will happen, and it will seem quicker if you concentrate on other things for the moment. Have lunch and a nice walk with a good friend.

Your Body

*Y*ou can prepare yourself for labor. Concentrate on the purpose of the contractions; allowing for the passage of the baby from the safe, restful womb. It is not an easy passage, so concentrate on relaxing your body, to let it do its work. You are flexible.

*K**eep up your energy with proper nourishment and comfortable walks. You need as much energy as the baby.*

_____

_____

_____

_____

*W**hat is the weather like on your walks these last weeks? Take the time to enjoy the fresh air and some leisure time.*

_____

_____

_____

The Tenth Month

The tenth month is a time of recovery and adjustment. Recovery from the labor and delivery, and recovery of yourself, the self you wondered if you would ever see again.

Now more than ever, it is important to continue exercising, just for yourself. With the birth of your baby you will immediately lose 10 - 15 pounds and another few quickly. Exercise will hasten the weight loss, and it will help keep up your spirits. It is normal to have short periods of crying and exhaustion just after your baby is born. You have accomplished something extraordinary and the magnitude of it is daunting.

Exercise can help improve your spirits while recovering your ideal figure. Don't worry or feel guilty about your baby ''blues.'' You'll

most likely feel better in ten days or so. You also need plenty of rest during these first weeks. Try to rest while your infant is sleeping, and let your partner help with household chores. Pregnancy is not an illness, but it consumes an enormous amount of energy.

The baby needs to adjust to you and you to it. A supportive partner's understanding now will help restore the status quo. In no time you'll wonder what your life was like before the baby was born.

The End Result

Place baby's photo here.

Name _____

Date of birth _____

Place of birth _____

Weight _____

Length _____

Parents _____